Weekend Fun

Let's Go to a
Play

By Mary Hill

Children's Press®
A Division of Scholastic Inc.
New York / Toronto / London / Auckland / Sydney
Mexico City / New Delhi / Hong Kong
Danbury, Connecticut

Photo Credits: Cover, p. 7 © Index Stock Imagery, Inc.; pp. 5, 9, 11, 19 Maura B. McConnell; p. 13 © Phil Banko/Corbis; p. 15 © Reuters NewMedia Inc./Corbis; p. 17 © Micheline Pelletier/Corbis
Contributing Editors: Shira Laskin and Jennifer Silate
Book Design: Michael DeLisio

Library of Congress Cataloging-in-Publication Data

Hill, Mary, 1977-
    Let's go to a play / by Mary Hill.
    p. cm.—(Weekend fun)
    Includes index.
    Summary: Describes the experiences of a young girl and her father when they go to a theater to see a play.
    ISBN 0-516-23995-3 (lib. bdg.)—ISBN 0-516-25919-9 (pbk.)
    1. Theater—Juvenile literature. [1. Theater.] I. Title. II. Series.

PN2037.H45 2003
792—dc21

                                                                2003009157

Contents

My name is Joanne.

My father and I are going to see a **play** tonight.

5

We will see the play in a **theater**.

The theater is big.

CATS
SPEED LIMIT 30
INTER GARDEN
CATS
Winter Garden
CATS NOW AND FOREVER
BIKE LANE ONLY

We go inside the theater.

An **usher** takes us to
our seats.

There are many seats in the theater.

The **curtain** opens when the play is about to begin.

The lights will go out, too.

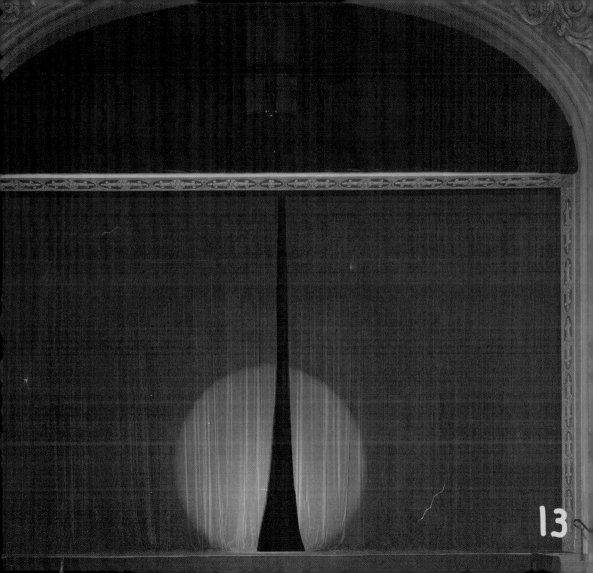

The actors come onstage.

The actors wear makeup and **costumes**.

The actors tell a story.

They **pretend** to be the **characters** in the play.

When the play ends,
we clap our hands.

That was a good play!

21

New Words

characters (**karik**-tuhrz) people in a story, book, play, movie, or television program

costumes (**kahs**-tooms) special clothing you put on so that you look like someone else

curtain (**kurt**-uhn) a piece of fabric pulled across a window or stage to cover it

play (**play**) a kind of story with people acting different parts

pretend (pri-**tend**) to say or act as if something that is not true is true

theater (**thee**-uh-tuhr) a place where movies or plays are seen

usher (**uhsh**-ur) someone who shows people to their seats in a theater

22

To Find Out More

Books
All the World's a Stage
by Rebecca Davidson
HarperCollins Children's Book Group

On Stage!: Theater Games and Activities for Kids
by Lisa Bany-Winters
Chicago Review Press

Web Site
Kids Work!
http://www.knowitall.org/kidswork/theater
Learn about the history of theater, the jobs you can do in a theater, and more on this Web site.

Index

About the Author

Mary Hill has written many books for children. For fun on the weekends, she likes to go sailing.

Reading Consultants

Kris Flynn, Coordinator, Small School District Literacy, The San Diego County Office of Education

Shelly Forys, Certified Reading Recovery Specialist, W.J. Zahnow Elementary School, Waterloo, IL

Paulette Mansell, Certified Reading Recovery Specialist, and Early Literacy Consultant, TX